THE SCIENCE OF A CUTBACK

NEL YOMTOV

Published in the United States of America by Cherry Lake Publishing
Ann Arbor, Michigan
www.cherrylakepublishing.com

Surfing Adviser: Ian Akahi Masterson, "The Surf Professor"
Physics Adviser: Mike Giromini, Director of Regional School Improvement and Accountability at Plymouth-Canton
Community Schools, former physics teacher and swim coach
Reading Adviser: Marla Conn, ReadAbility, Inc.

Photo Credits: © Kazunori Sano | Dreamstime.com, cover, 1; © trubavin/Shutterstock Images, 5, 15; © Sebastien Burel/
Shutterstock.com, 6; © Zoonar/Thinkstock Images, 9, 13; © Everett Collection/Shutterstock Images, 10; © Markus
Gebauer/Shutterstock.com, 12; © Friday | Dreamstime.com - Surfer In Ocean Photo, 16; © Fouroaks | Dreamstime.com -
Surfing Wipeout Photo, 19; © Trubavin | Dreamstime.com - Surfing Photo, 20; © Devy | Dreamstime.com - VALE
FIGUEIRAS, PORTUGAL - Surfers Getting Surf Classes Photo, 22; © Friday | Dreamstime.com - Pending Waves Photo, 25;
© Mana Photo/Shutterstock.com, 26; © Blend Images/Thinkstock Images, 28

Library of Congress Cataloging-in-Publication Data

Yomtov, Nelson.
  The science of a cutback/Nel Yomtov.
     pages cm.—(Full-Speed Sports)
  Includes webography.
  Includes bibliographical references and index.
  Audience: Age: 8–12.
  Audience: Grade: 4 to 6.
  ISBN 978-1-63362-581-5 (hardcover)—ISBN 978-1-63362-761-1 (pdf)—ISBN 978-1-63362-671-3 (paperback)—
ISBN 978-1-63362-851-9 (ebook)
  1. Surfing—Juvenile literature. 2. Sports sciences—Juvenile literature. I. Title.

  GV840.S8Y66 2015
  797.3'2—dc23
                        2015005836

Cherry Lake Publishing would like to acknowledge the work of
the Partnership for 21st Century Skills. Please visit *www.p21.org*
for more information.

Printed in the United States of America
Corporate Graphics

ABOUT THE AUTHOR

Nel Yomtov is an award-winning author of nonfiction books and graphic novels for young readers.
He lives in the New York City area.

TABLE OF CONTENTS

CHAPTER 1

RIDING THE WAVES!

Cherise and her mother walked along the beach in Southern California. She watched as one surfer girl got into a low crouch and began moving across the **face** of the wave. At the same time, she made a T shape with her arms. Then she reached down and touched the water with her left hand. As she kept moving, she turned to look behind her at the white foam along the top part of the wave, called **whitewater**. Suddenly, in a sharp, twisting motion, the surfer turned her board completely around and moved back *toward* the wave!

"Why is she doing *that?*" Cherise asked.

"She wants to get back to the power of the wave," said her mother. "When she does, she'll turn around again and surf the wave back toward the shore. It's called a **cutback**, because the surfer cuts back to the wave."

"Maybe I can learn that someday," Cherise said.

"It's a difficult **maneuver**," her mom said. "But with a lot of practice, I know you'll be great at it!"

A cutback is a difficult but popular surfing maneuver.

Surfers need to use hydrodynamic forces to their advantage.

A cutback is a complete 180-degree change of direction in which the surfer turns all the way back into the wave before completing his or her ride. It requires speed, skill, good technique—and science, in the form of certain **forces** of nature.

The cutback became popular during the 1970s, when modern surfboards became shorter and more maneuverable. But surfers have been cutting back into the wave for as long as waves have been ridden. In fact, the origins of surfing date back thousands of years, with many songs about **heʻe nalu**, or surfing. A traditional Hawaiian story describes a cutback as "Heʻeana i ka wai ʻololi ho ʻi ana i ka wai ʻolola" (surfing into the narrow waters and returning onto the wide part of the wave). People on Pacific islands had a strong understanding of **hydrodynamic** forces, or how water moves—which was essential to how they survived and thrived.

GO DEEPER!

Read this chapter again. What is the main idea? What is a cutback? How long have surfers performed cutbacks? What elements contribute to performing a cutback? Is science involved in making the cutback turn?

CHAPTER 2

THE ORIGINS OF SURFING

The exact origins of surfing remain a mystery, but historians know fishermen in Peru rode waves on reed boats called *cabillitos* about 5,000 years ago. In ancient Polynesia—a group of more than 1,000 islands in the Pacific Ocean—surfing was a basic skill learned by children and mastered by oceanic voyagers who brought surfing to Hawaii over 2,000 years ago.

By about 1000 CE, surfing had become a national pastime in both Tahiti and the Hawaiian Islands. People often surfed at religious celebrations. Many high-ranking

Children in ancient Polynesia learned to surf, and the sport is still popular with young people today.

chiefs and chiefesses were strong, fearless surfers, which demonstrated their leadership qualities.

In 1779, Lieutenant James King, an officer on the British ship *Discovery*, wrote description of Hawaiian surfing in the ship's **log**. He was just one of many Europeans fascinated by surfing. "Where there is a very great sea, and the surf breaking on the shore," wrote King, "the men push forward with their arms to keep on its top, it sends them in with a most astonishing velocity, and the great art is to guide the plank so as

In the 1930s, surfing started to become popular in California.

always to keep it in a proper direction."

As boatloads of Europeans settled in Hawaii and Polynesia in the 1800s, rapid changes took place. As native people moved **inland** to the growing cities, they left their surfboards behind. Colonists and **missionaries** encouraged the local people to adopt Western customs, learn English, and give up the dangerous sport of surfing. By the late-1800s, visitors observed that hardly anyone was riding the waves offshore in Waikiki. Meanwhile, at a school in California, three Hawaiian princes hewed their own surfboards out of redwood, and rode the cold waves of the West Coast.

Interest in the sport began to grow again in the early 1900s. George Freeth, born in Hawaii to an Irish father and Polynesian-Hawaiian mother, was one of the leading surfers at Waikiki Beach. Jack London, the author of *Call of the Wild*, observed Freeth surfing in 1907. Soon, he wrote an article in a popular American magazine describing the talented athlete and the wonders of surfing. Interest in the sport began to soar in the United States.

In 1908, the journalist Alexander Ford Hume helped establish the very successful Outrigger Canoe Club in Waikiki, which promoted the surfing lifestyle. Duke Kahanamoku, a member of the Outrigger, helped establish the Hui Nalu club. "The Duke" had a passion for surfing and had a desire to share this lifestyle with people all around the world. From the 1910s to 1930s, he demonstrated surfing in places like England, Australia,

Performing a cutback without falling requires good balance.

LOOK!

Look at how this surfer has positioned his body. Reread chapter 1. Does it look like he's performing a cutback correctly? Make a guess about how he's keeping his balance. Continue on to chapter 3 to see if you're right.

and New Zealand. This "ambassador of **aloha**" helped surfing become extremely popular.

The origin of the cutback dates back to the beginnings of surfing. But since the global explosion of surfing occurred in the 1960s, thousands of surfers around the world have developed new techniques, to use the forces of nature to their advantage.

A statue of Duke Kahanamoku stands today in Waikiki.

CHAPTER 3

THE SCIENCE OF THE CUTBACK

The two main physical forces at work upon the surfer and his board are **gravity** and **buoyancy**. Gravity is the force that pulls all objects—people, mountains, trees, the moon, and everything else—*downward* toward Earth. Buoyancy is a force created by water pushing *upward* on an object. In surfing, the water beneath the board **exerts** its force on all parts of the board that it touches.

Gravity and buoyancy are opposing forces. When a surfer is standing or lying down at the center of the surfboard in calm water, the forces are in balance and

Gravity and buoyancy work together to keep the surfer balanced on his or her board.

things are stable. When he moves backward on the board or shifts his weight backward, the gravity also shifts. But because the buoyancy is still distributed evenly across the board, the front of the board tips upward, and the back of the board sinks under his feet.

Once the ride begins, hydrodynamics act upon the surfer and the board. The continuous motions of the water push and pull the surfboard. To steer and ride the waves, a surfer works with these forces by leaning and shifting his weight side to side and front to back.

The surfer positions his arms out to his sides to keep his balance.

To perform a cutback, the surfer first crouches as he surfs along the face of the wave, while making a T shape with his arms. This way, he can lean the board to one side and reach down to touch the water with his hand, which will slow him down. He holds the opposite arm up in the air to create a counterbalance.

The surfer then continues to lean inward and forcefully pivots around the hand touching the water. This maneuver begins to turn the surfer back to the whitewater of the wave. At this point, he starts to come out of the deep crouch position. The surfer keeps his eyes on his target—the whitewater—at all times.

When he reaches the whitewater, he throws up his arms so he can climb the wave as high as possible. This lets him turn around again and use the power of the wave to continue forward with speed and flow.

A smooth cutback is more than just a flashy trick. A cutback also helps the surfer get back on the face of the wave to reuse its energy, at full speed. With proper training, surfing can be very safe. But there are plenty of dangers for surfers of all ages and skill levels to keep in mind.

THINK ABOUT IT!

Now that you understand a bit about gravity and buoyancy, do you think it would be possible to surf without those forces at work? Why or why not? On a piece of paper, draw an ocean wave and show the path made in the water by a surfer performing a cutback.

CHAPTER 4

SURFERS BEWARE!

Scientists, sports medicine doctors, and experienced surfers warn about the many potential dangers of surfing. Smart surfers, however, will make ocean safety their top priority each time they venture out into the waters.

Large ocean waves are among the most powerful forces in nature and are a very real threat to a surfer's safety. An average 10-foot (3 meter) wave weighs thousands of tons, and that force of gravity pushing down on a surfer can cause serious injury. A surfer who falls from the surfboard into the water can be swept along the rough, sandy bottom of the seabed. Broken bones, bruises, cuts, fractures, and sprains are common surfing injuries. Drowning is also an ever-present danger. Experts strongly recommend you always surf with a friend who can help you if you get into trouble.

Falling off a surfboard can be very dangerous.

Sometimes, waves are strong enough to break a surfboard in half.

A **rip current** is a fast-moving ocean current that pulls people and objects toward the open sea, away from the beach. Surfers who wipe out can be swept out to sea further than they can swim back to shore. If you ever get caught in a rip current, don't try to swim against it. Instead, swim across the current towards the **breakers** so that they can wash you back towards the shore. The important thing is not to panic. Even treading water until the rip current subsides is better than trying to swim against it.

The surfboard itself also poses the threat of injury. Not only is the front end of a board pointed, but modern surfboards have one or more sharp-edged fins on their bottoms. The fins help improve stability and foot-steering control of the board. A wave can hurl the board into a surfer who has wiped out, or toss it into the air where it becomes a dangerous flying object to other surfers in the area.

Another threat to surfers is the marine life lurking in the ocean. Seals, sea snakes, jellyfish, and stingrays can cause painful wounds or bites that can be potentially life-threatening. Shark attacks on surfers

GO DEEPER!

Think about what you've read in this chapter. What kind of dangers might someone encounter in the ocean? What advice would you give a surfer who wanted to ride the waves safely?

In a surf class, you can learn some good techniques and safety tips.

are extremely rare, but they can be one of the most frightening and nightmarish experiences any surfer can have. However, many native Pacific Islanders respected sharks as friendly, wise ancestral spirits, so rather than showing fear, surfers who encounter sharks should "show aloha" and leave them alone.

Before paddling out to catch the waves, smart surfers follow a few basic safety rules. Spend time on the beach observing the conditions and the people in the water, and plan your exit before you jump into the water. Be aware of other surfers and of the surf conditions, such as the strength of the waves or unseen rip currents. Surf only in waves in which you are comfortable. Make sure you are physically fit when surfing and are capable of swimming back to shore in case you wipe out. By following a few simple safety tips, you should be safe in the surf.

CHAPTER 5

THE BOARD'S THE THING

Surfboards can be found in all shapes and sizes. They are usually grouped together by their basic shape and how they are best used. For cutbacks and other tight turns, many advanced surfers use the shortboard. Today's shortboard typically measures between 6 and 7 feet (1.8 m and 2.1 m) long, with a pointed front and rounded or squarish tail. By comparison, longboards range from 8 to 12 feet (2.4 m to 3.6 m) long. Most shortboards have either three or four fins, but some have as many as five. Surfboards have changed over

Modern surfboards, like this one, usually have pointed tips.

A surfboard's light but sturdy materials are perfect for making quick turns.

the years as shapers and surfers have learned more about the hydrodynamics of surfing.

The shorter length of the shortboard allows surfers to make quick, aggressive turns and perform dazzling cutbacks and other showy maneuvers. By using a minimal amount of the construction materials, such as fiberglass and **resin**, a shortboard is also built to be thin and light.

Australian surfer Nat Young is regarded as one of the pioneers of the shortboard. In 1966, Young rode a shorter, thinner board to win the World Surfing

Championships in San Diego, pulling off harder and sharper turns than any of his competitors. Californian George Greenough and Australians Bob McTavish and Wayne Lynch further popularized the shortboard. By the 1970s, the shortboard revolution was in full swing, and the board had become the favorite choice of most professional surfers.

THINK ABOUT IT!

Competitive surfing is a very popular sport in many parts of the world. What are the positive and negative aspects of competitive sports? Do the positives—both physical and emotional—outweigh the negatives? Are sports worth the time commitment and potential threat of injury?

Surfers get "stoked" about the ocean waves.

Surfing is a fun and enjoyable sport, and is one of the most popular board sports ever invented. Riding a wave is a breathtaking experience and a great way to get away from the stresses of school and work. Each wave you surf is a different experience, each one offering a unique feeling that only a surfer knows. In fact, surfers agree that surfing makes you feel alive and brings you closer to nature—the ocean, sun, and sand of a gorgeous beach. The Duke understood well that at the root of surfing is a spirit of aloha. Surfers who ride a good wave feel "stoked!"

TIMELINE

A TIMELINE HISTORY OF SURFING

Circa 3000 BCE	Fishermen in Peru ride waves on seahorse-shaped boats made of reeds.
3000 BCE to 1000 CE	Stand-up surfing appears in Polynesia.
1000 CE	Surfing takes hold in the Hawaiian Islands as a popular sport and for fishing.
1779	Lieutenant James King records accounts of Hawaiians surfing on boards made from different materials.
Early 1800s	Western colonialism and urbanization in Hawaii causes islanders to give up their native customs; by the mid-1800s, surfing almost completely disappears from Hawaii and most other Pacific islands.
1907	Irish-Hawaiian George Freeth arrives in Southern California to give lessons in surfing.
1908	Alexander Ford Hume establishes a surfing club in Waikiki, Hawaii.
1910s–1930s	Hawaii-born Duke Kahanamoku introduces surfing to Australia, New Zealand, the West and East Coasts of the United States, and other places.
1950s–present	Surfing becomes a worldwide sensation; lighter and more stable boards allow riders to perform new tricks and maneuvers, such as the cutback; manufacturers experiment with different surfboard shapes and high-tech materials.

THINK ABOUT IT

Read chapter 3 again. What are two of the major physical forces acting upon the surfer in the water? How does each affect the surfer? What are hydro-dynamic forces? Give a step-by-step description of the cutback turn.

Go online with an adult and watch a video clip of someone surfing. Or find and watch a movie about surfing: try the classic documentary *The Endless Summer*, or the drama *Soul Surfer*, based on the true story of Bethany Hamilton. Would you ever try surf-ing yourself? Why or why not? Which things would be the best parts? Which things would be the hardest?

Name a few highlights in the history of surfing. Do scientists know exactly who the first ancient surfers were? Where did surfing become extremely popular in around the year 1000? Name the three individuals who helped the growth of the sport in Hawaii.

Reread chapter 5. Why is the size and shape of the surfboard so important for performing a cutback? What might happen if it were bigger or smaller?

LEARN MORE

FURTHER READING

Mason, Paul. *Surfing: The World's Most Fantastic Surf Spots and Techniques.*
Mankato, MN: Capstone Press, 2011.

Moser, Patrick. *Pacific Passages: An Anthology of Surf Writing.* Honolulu, HI:
University of Hawaii Press, 2008.

Rusch, Elizabeth. *The Next Wave: The Quest to Harness the Power of the Oceans.*
Boston: Houghton Mifflin Harcourt, 2014.

WEB SITES

Ducksters—Extreme: Surfing
www.ducksters.com/sports/extremesurfing.php
Get a handle on surfing basics, equipment, and common surfing terms.

Enchanted Learning—All About Ocean and Seas
www.enchantedlearning.com/subjects/ocean/Waves.shtml
Learn what causes waves and uncover lots more information about the mysteries of
Earth's oceans.

How Stuff Works—How Surfing Works
www.howstuffworks.com/outdoor-activities/water-sports/surfing.htm
Get the inside scoop on the history of surfing and the latest developments in surfboards and surfing gear.

Science Wire—The Science of Surfing
www.exploratorium.edu/theworld/surfing/physics/
Learn about the science of breaking waves, surfing, and controlling a surfboard.

GLOSSARY

aloha (uh-LOH-hah) in Hawaiian, a term used to say hello or goodbye, or love, peace, compassion, and/or forgiveness

breakers (BRAY-kurz) large sea waves that break into white foam as they reach the shore

buoyancy (BOI-yan-see) the upward force on an object in a fluid

cutback (KUHT-bak) a complete 180-degree change of direction in which the surfer turns all the way back into the wave behind him or her

exerts (ig-ZURTZ) applies a force to make something happen

face (FASE) the steep shoreward-facing front of a wave

forces (FORS-sez) any actions that produce, stop, or change the shape or movement of an object

gravity (GRAV-ih-tee) the force that pulls things toward the center of the earth and keeps them from floating away

he'e nalu (HEH-eh NAH-loo) a Hawaiian term for surfing

hydrodynamic (hye-droh-dye-NAM-ik) dealing with the forces exerted by fluids in motion

inland (IN-luhnd) located away from the sea

log (LAHG) a written record of what happens on a ship's voyage, kept by the captain or another officer

maneuver (muh-NOO-vur) a difficult movement that requires planning and skill

missionaries (MISH-uh-ner-eez) people sent to a foreign country to teach about religion and do good works

resin (REZ-in) a sticky substance that oozes from some trees and plants that is used to make plastics and varnishes

rip current (RIP KUR-uhnt) a fast-moving ocean current that pulls people and objects toward the open sea

whitewater (WITE-waw-tur) the frothy foam on the tops of breakers

INDEX

[21ST CENTURY SKILLS LIBRARY]